WHEN AND WHY DID THE HORSE FLY?

Knowing and Using Question Words

by Cari Meister

illustrated by Marek Jagucki

PICTURE WINDOW BOOKS
a capstone imprint

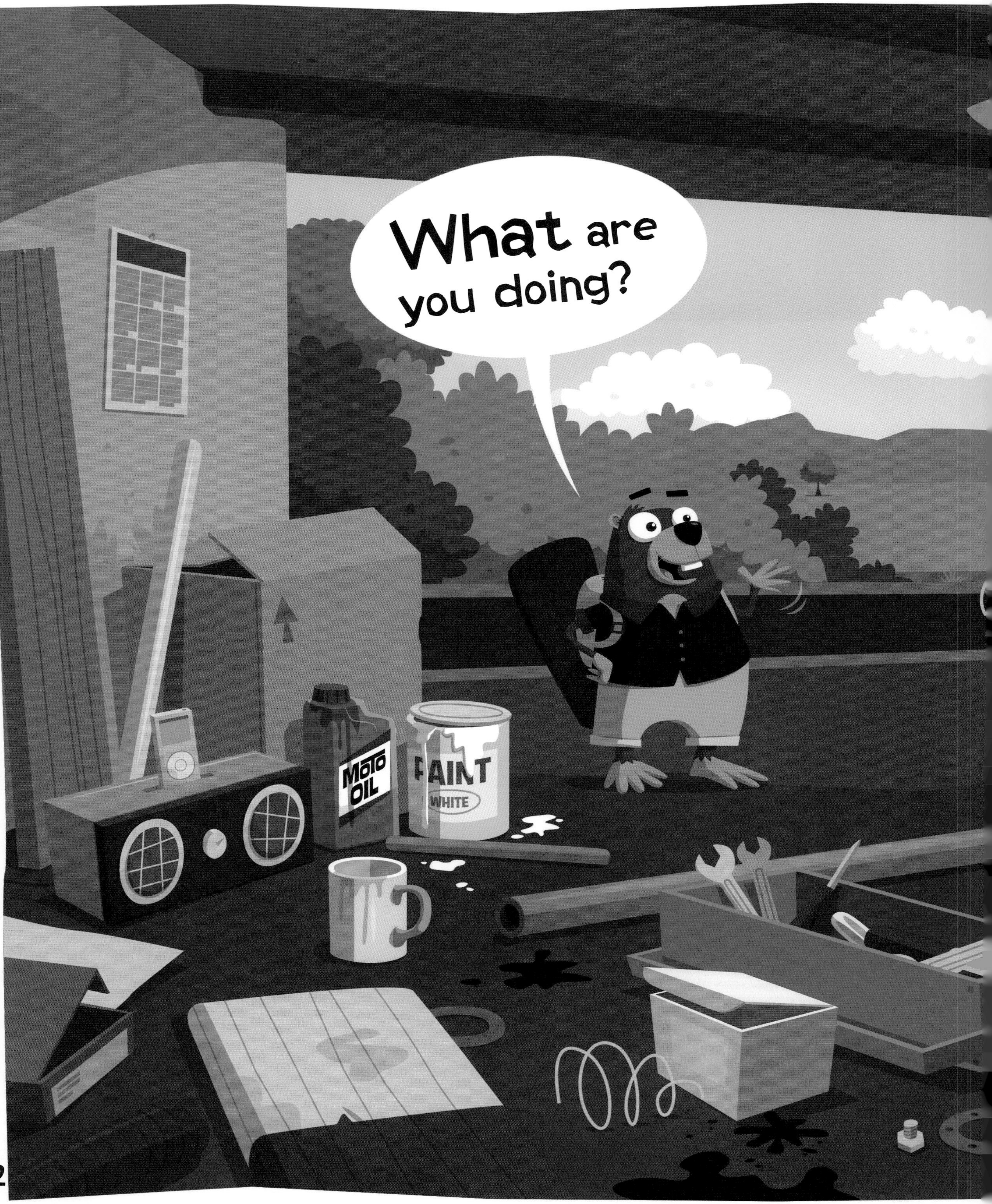
What are you doing?
MOTO OIL
PAINT
WHITE

How does it work?

See this button? You push it.

See this lever? You pull it.

See this pedal? You step on it.

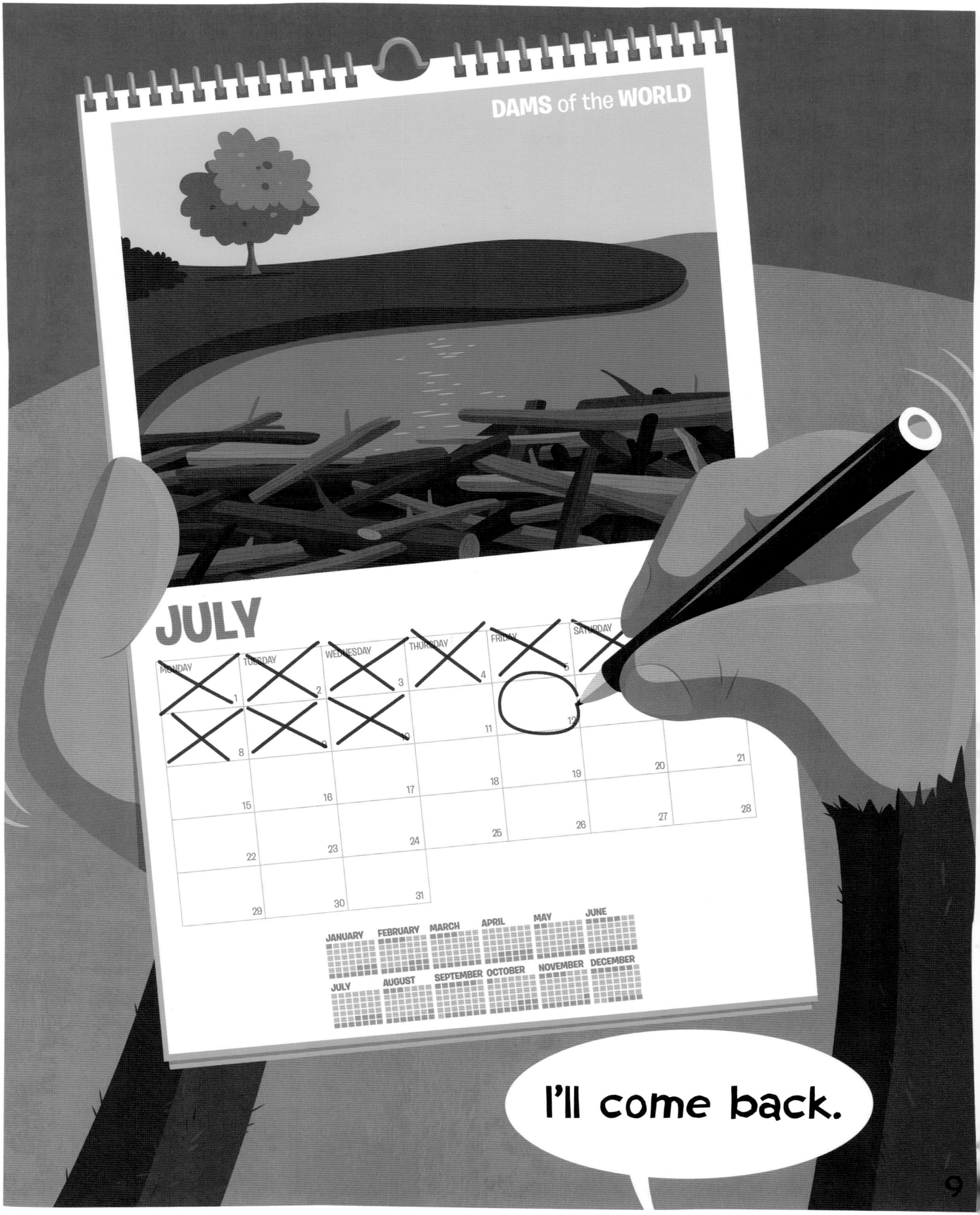
DAMS of the WORLD
JULY
I'll come back.

14

CLICK!

CLUNK!

CLACK!

About Question Words

What's one of the best ways to get information? Ask a question! The six main question words are *where, who, when, why, what,* and *how.* Answers to these question words supply information beyond "yes" or "no." Question words are also called interrogatives.

WHERE When a question uses the word *where,* the answer will always be a place. Where did it happen? At the grocery store. New York City. On a boat.

WHO When a question uses the word *who,* the answer will be a person or animal. Who did it? The doctor did it. Tia did it. The donkey did it.

WHEN When a question uses the word *when,* the answer will always be a time. It may be an exact time, such as "3:30" or "midnight." Or it may be a more general time, such as "after dinner."

WHY When a question uses the word *why,* the answer must include a reason. Why did you eat all the cookies? I ate all the cookies because I was hungry.

WHAT *What* is a very common question word. Depending on the question, there can be many different answers.
Question: What is his name?
Answer: Jorge.
Question: What does he do?
Answer: He swims.

HOW When a question uses the word *how,* the answer usually includes an explanation or instructions. It can also include a measurement.
Question: How do you make toast?
Answer: First you put a slice of bread in the toaster. Then you press down the lever.
Question: How long will it take?
Answer: About a minute.

Now you know all about question words. WHAT do you want to learn about next?

Read More

Cleary, Brian P. *Thumbtacks, Earwax, Lipstick, Dipstick: What Is a Compound Word?* Words Are CATegorical. Minneapolis: Millbrook Press, 2011.

Lichtenheld, Tom, and Ezra Fields-Meyer. *E-mergency!* San Francisco: Chronicle Books, 2011.

MacCuish, Al. *Operation Alphabet.* New York: Thames & Hudson, 2011.

Walton, Rick. *Just Me and 6,000 Rats: An Adventure in Conjunctions.* Layton, Utah: Gibbs Smith, 2011.

Special thanks to our adviser, Terry Flaherty, PhD, Professor of English, Minnesota State University, Mankato, for his expertise.

Editor: Jill Kalz
Designer: Lori Bye
Art Director: Nathan Gassman
Production Specialist: Kathy McColley
The illustrations in this book were created digitally.

Picture Window Books are published by Capstone,
1710 Roe Crest Drive, North Mankato, Minnesota 56003
www.capstonepub.com

Library of Congress Cataloging-in-Publication Data
Meister, Cari.
  When and why did the horse fly? : Knowing and using question words / By Cari Meister.
     pages cm. -- (Nonfiction picture books. Language on the loose.)
  Summary: "Introduces the question words How, What, When, Where, Who, and Why through the telling of an original story"—Provided by publisher.
  ISBN 978-1-4048-8319-2 (library binding)
  ISBN 978-1-4795-1918-7 (paperback)
  ISBN 978-1-4795-1905-7 (eBook PDF)
1. English language—Interrogative—Juvenile literature. 2. Language arts (Elementary) I. Title.

PE1395.M45 2014
   428.2—dc23   2013008066

Printed in the United States of America
in North Mankato, Minnesota.
032013   007223CGF13

Internet Sites

FactHound offers a safe, fun way to find Internet sites related to this book. All of the sites on FactHound have been researched by our staff.

Here's all you do:

Visit *www.facthound.com*

Type in this code: 9781404883192

Super-cool stuff! Check out projects, games and lots more at www.capstonekids.com

Look for all the books in the series:

Frog. Frog? Frog!
Understanding Sentence Types

Monsters Can Mosey
Understanding Shades of Meaning

whatever says mark
Knowing and Using Punctuation

When and Why Did the Horse Fly?
Knowing and Using Question Words